POLLING DATA AS A MEANS OF SELF-EXPRESSION

HAIKU BY TIMOTHY TARKELLY

OAC
BOOKS
OSAGE ARTS COMMUNITY

OAC Books
Belle, MO

OAC
BOOKS
OSAGE ARTS COMMUNITY

Copyright (c) Timothy Tarkelly, 2022
First Edition 1 3 5 7 9 10 8 6 4 2
ISBN: 98-1-958182-15-4
LCCN: 2022942430

Author photo: Janae Crowl

Acknowledgments:

For Terry,

Good son of Texas,
he's writing in Ron Paul's name
on heaven's ballots.

TABLE OF CONTENTS

On Liberty & Her Uglier Siblings

On Founding Documents and Floundering Fathers

On Liberty & Her Uglier Siblings

"The thing worse than rebellion is the thing that causes rebellion."

-Frederick Douglass

SAME PLAGUE DIFFERENT WITCH DOCTOR

Right or wrong, we march.
Ad hominem sage bundles
burn to clear the vibes.

DOOM SCROLLING

Dire wolf vanguards
pontificating love and war
in comment sections.

ELECTION SEASON ON CAMPUS

Tables fill the quad.
Pamphlets meekly tossed into
purple trash cans.

EUROPEAN SOLIDARITY

A hushed hemisphere
watches the bombs fall and waves
blue and yellow flags.

RBG

A brave stamp dissents.
Ivy league scrutiny flares
in public chambers.

SETH CORDELL FOR GOVERNOR

Kansans deal in work,
fields they can harvest themselves,
friends who do the same.

AOC

Soundbites summon hate.
Facebook dads tongue fuck the void,
pin their blame on youth.

MARCH 5TH, 2016

Caucus captains wake
to the promise of sure things.
Bauble pins and tears.

CONWAY

Yard signs don't get votes,
volume does. Grit and panic.
Frighten your neighbors.

WE SHOT MALCOLM X

Resolve takes the stage.
Rage burns hotter when it's right,
scares the folks at home.

ALL THE HOMESTEADS ARE TAKEN

Stand at the boat ramp,
sing Emersonian hymns
to the stocked sunfish.

BASED POLITICS

For Hannah and Brad

Nuance radio.
Smooth tones simmer as they give
takes so hot, so based.

SOUTHERN CROSS

Slow fading colors.
Heritage is a weird word
for memory loss.

SUNDAY FLIGHTS

Representatives
grab the wrong bags, leave ethics
back in their districts.

THE DAY WE ALMOST JOINED THE MODERN WHIG PARTY

for TJ

Brown ale lubricates
unwitting voices, free thought,
and freer markets.

MONTICELLO

Noble gadgetry
at the seat of Southern charm,
its humid solace.

BOSTON TEA PARTY

Property exiled
by weak tropes and performance,
wasteful bouts of rage.

SECOND DEPLOYMENT

She came back sleepless,
her last strips of childhood tied
to Baghdad's skyline.

CAPITOL BUILDING

Built from bonded hands.
Stately posture, bold marble,
engraved retractions.

JANUARY 6TH

A mob of free men
pissing on crypts carved by slaves.
The networks make bank.

GORSUCH

Assess as written.
Facts are neither cold nor hard,
they handle with ease.

MISS KANSAS

Wears her politics
on the inside of her sleeve.
Just does the right thing.

ANGELA

Reset the dials.
Actions drown out mere platforms,
out-shout the haters.

SPIKE

Carry your own torch,
strike flint at the Waffle House.
You are the power!

ABIGAIL

Patient love and ink.
Nuptial stationery
exerting hearts home.

JESSE VENTURA

Out of town money
and cameo demagogues
can't stop history.

SANDRA BLAND

Innocence flatlines.
We willfully dodge the news,
we forget her name.

PRESS CORPS

Pundits paid in full,
the dinner circuit darlings
will print anything.

REPLY STOP TO UNSUBSCRIBE

Call to inaction:
wiki-activists resist
learning on your own!

A PEACEFUL TRANSFER OF POWER

Exemplar hearts know
departing quietly brings
a thunderous death.

NORTHSTAR CAUCUS

Well-meaning desk hand
holds a Menshevik prayer book,
big ideas on greed.

ON ESTABLISHMENTS AND UNDRAINED SWAMPS

Career politicians
throw rocks in glass limousines
bought with donations.

VETERANS AFFAIRS

Achilles brown bags it,
takes coins in Lafayette Park,
sleeps the day away.

MUIR'S YELLOWSTONE

> All a good cause needs
> is a poet, scotch bottles,
> some eager ears.

MARTHA

Warm hearts always greet
new daughters first. Affection
gives scenery depth.

ON DE GAUL COMPLEXES AND VAIN SECRETS

> Ohioans count,
> on one arthritic finger,
> the men they can trust.

NITP

Nostalgic names hatch
into faceless beasts, snarling
heads up their asses.

ANTI-FEDERALIST PAPERS

Roman archetypes
and modern wisdom prevails.
Truth's most veiled bulwark.

BRUTUS X

Street corner sentries.
History's faithless pages
overrun with horror.

CULT OF PERSONALITY

Idols fester until
a fear of adulation
awakes the godly.

EXEGESIS

I like amendments
like I like my innate rights:
enumerated.

POLLING DATA AS A MEANS OF SELF-EXPRESSION

Houses can't divide.
That's something else: rootless ground,
partisan nonsense.

PRESIDENTIAL PROCLAMATION TERMINATING EXECUTIVE ORDER 9066

Call it tradition.
Freedom's the thing with feathers
we've always kept caged.

EXECUTIVE ORDER 11905

A new moral ground.
Base impulses banned forthwith.
Clarify later.

FIFTY-STATE STRATEGY

Dare us to agree.
Patriots love a challenge,
short election nights.

SOUL ON ICE

Hardback heroes framed
in books bound from strife, violence.
Read with the lights on.

SHELTER IN PLACE

The mandates emerge
to mixed reviews, stilted talk.
See you in four weeks.

REMEMBER WHEN POLITICS WERE CIVILIZED?

Peace is a mirage
long since shattered by old men,
Aaron Burr's bullets.

Y'ALL CAN GO TO HELL, I'M GOING TO TEXAS

Andy Jackson's soul
rots on the Etowah shore.
So much for old friends.

KETANJI BROWN JACKSON I

Gold stamped resumes
blight beneath virtue charades,
ruined by spotlights.

KETANJI BROWN JACKSON II

Validation sails.
Civil regard and due praise
chill in the soft wake.

NATHANAEL GREENE

Meeting house or war?
In a heart so stout, which chamber
do the ears hear first?

OCCUPY THE OCCUPY MOVEMENT

Striplings step en force.
Constructive criticism
knows no painted signs.

NPS

Places like Pecos
deserve gentle hands and deep coffers,
belong to us all.

BLOOMBERG

Man cannot live by
name recognition alone.
Just once, say something.

OPERATION CONDOR

Alibis combust.
Espiocrats sell slogans
in local tender.

WRITE IN FICUS

Photosynthesis
is the only thing I trust.
Make sugar, not war.

GREEN HERRING

Kyle says save the cows,
trucks almond milk cross country,
vacations in Spain.

NORTH COUNTRY

The French can't resist
studied naturalism,
Iroquois blessings.

THE AMERICAN RANCHER

Lariat ethics,
men who shape dry acreage,
divine sweat from sand.

APOCALYPSE EQUATION

Stochastic pencils
tell us what we've always known:
peace fails at gunpoint.

WE ARE CORN PEOPLE

Native soil brings fruit.
Ethanol, decent whiskey
get the heart thumping.

SIT-ROOM

Scales freshly zeroed,
proportional responses
flash with neon joy.

GITMO

Barbed wire and damp fear.
Due process in a tight veil,
waiting for its day.

MIKE GRAVEL, 2008

Blue-blood theatre.
All those lights, but no airtime.
Careers flayed in vain.

SNOWDEN

Conflicting oaths push
stalwart men to reason's edge,
force heroes to hide.

HALDEMAN I

Clears his throat to speak.
Acousmatic orchestras
wind their slickened strings.

THE JUNIOR REPRESENTATIVE

Shared office spaces.
The machine itself at work
behind brass placards.

MITCH

Corn cracker solon,
eats any district he wants,
vitriol for lunch.

MOUNT VERNON

Antique fixtures drip
every known shade of green,
decay in real time.

PATRIOT ACT

Clever names overrule
discarded declarations
turned into nooses.

HALDEMAN II

Suit pocket zippo sparks,
lights public particulars.
Cigar smoke and film.

NATIONAL ARCHIVES

Waited half a day.
Cried at the Magna Carta,
faded Bill of Rights.

SHORT STRAW RESUMPTION

Fresh prosperity
comes with receipts, lenders drooling
at every gate.

THE STATE

The same hand that feeds
puts on black body armor,
puts kids in cages.

JOHN EDWARDS

My first donation
spoiled on a head of hair,
failed family man.

BOB BARR, 2008

First vote done just right,
a former suit cleanly pressed,
subversive swagger.

GARY JOHNSON, 2012

A mail-in ballot
and a victor's stroke of pride
sing true. I'm all in.

GARY JOHNSON, 2016

Foreign capitals
don't even need to be named.
Just keep the tanks home.

CLINTONISTA

At least I fell hard,
blue leaflets and warmer friends
knocking doors with hope.

RED FISTS AND EMPTY TORCHES

We all need to go left,
feel the cool winds of justice
before they fail us.

2020

Lesser evils still
speak Hades' sulfurous tongue.
I want my vote back.

LIB-SOC

Quixotic rail ties:
porcupine philosophy,
blue union labels.

THE BUST ON MY WINDOW SILL

Stuck on consensus,
I'll chant Rousseau in my wet dreams
and never get up.

FREE STATE

Jayhawkers ready,
keeping Missouri at bay
for two hundred years.

JILL STEIN RUNS AGAIN

Encore performance.
Dull lights and silent cheers
abound, move right on.

GORBACHEV

Old worlds, new causes.
Port wine stains, birthmarks
giving levity.

FREE EXERCISE THEREOF

Pitchforks assemble,
as long as they don't make hay
out of congressmen.

2A

A standing army
and loaded meanings. Words bare
self-regulation.

ON CRYING AT THE UN HEADQUARTERS

A step toward hope.
Saint George guards the East River
so we don't have to.

HALEY

Adverse insight speaks.
Respect's a slippery slope,
only slides one way.

THE PEACE SUMMIT FALLS APART

Two-state solutions:
chickens laid by eggs, missiles,
calligraphed homelands.

CAMBODIA, 1970

Black swamp strategists,
borders written in pencil.
No regrets needed.

SECURITY COUNCIL

Jungle gym bullies
push non-permanent members
on old rusty swings.

AGGRESSIVE POSTURE

The high ground caves in.
Bigger sticks rule the table.
Moral avalanche.

ALAMO

The brave line thins out.
Legends melt into ghosthood,
pervading anthems.

TEXAS OIL BOOM

New age carpet bags.
Emetic fumes waft Westward,
buy up blackened ground.

THE FORT UNION BOYS

Bacon and whiskey.
The only pieces of home
that can stand the heat.

BARBARY

Latent terms of war.
House arrest diplomats
take on the ocean.

INTERNET OF THINGS

Bezos takes credit,
says he invented friendship,
gives it a soft voice.

CHURCH COMMITTEE

Ad lib at the mic,
emphatic fists of sulfur
burning podiums.

JUDAS OF THE WEST

Henry clay sits at cards,
losing. His loose, wine stained lips
collecting favors.

HOLLISTER WILDLIFE AREA

Public hunting land,
the right to hike with a gun,
no game for miles.

DRED SCOTT V. SANFORD

Audacious hatred.
Tyranny as a favor
we'll never pay back.

BURLINGTON TURNCOAT FACTORY

Team player, my ass.
Party platforms are kindling
for comeback campaigns.

THE REPUBLIC

Chairs stripped of cushions,
gavels too heavy to lift
without a pure heart.

PRIVILEGE

Wish away the guilt,
congenital influence,
poisonous forebears.

JOHN MCAFEE'S BOAT PULLS IN

The ledger hawks perch,
foam from their sharp beaks and feed
at liberty's shore.

SIC SEMPER DOCTORES

A bandaged nation
needs justice, doctors who dare
set the traitor's leg.

ANONYMOUSLY

Cyberverse zealots
throwing sharp stones at spy cams,
feigning ignorance.

NSA

Five Eyes got me shook.
Cancel all correspondence,
well-meaning emails.

FAUCET MINES

Digital pickaxe
swings at old monopolies,
unearths raw fortune.

BATTLE FLAGS

White washed butcher rags
offer peace dove pine branches,
appeals to Heaven.

PEACEFIELD

Idyllic dirt farm.
Unitarian prayer
and dull longings bloom.

SECOND INDOCHINA WAR

Black and white broadcasts
of jungle flora, our sons
a whole globe away.

ON SCARES, RED OR OTHERWISE

Wanton brats grow bold,
voir dire with Miss Liberty,
and digress at home.

BUMPER STICKER BLUES

A doctrine cocktail:
coiled snakes and thin blue lines?
Polar opposites.

VOLUNTEERS

Can't lead the wild.
The leatherstocking madmen
think they built this land.

2003

Scenes of shock-and awe,
footage by the bloody yard
followed by reruns.

MOOSEHEAD

Canoes as lanterns,
lights that bring new country folk
to wooded altars.

DEMOCRATIC CENTRALISM

Big thought puppeteers.
Hyperbolic at its best,
probably a lie.

ROE V. WADE

[Text hereby removed.
Author's lack of uterus
outshines all his thoughts.]

TWO IF BY SEA

The yellow bellies,
fattened calves of Kent, red coats,
red meat are coming.

AGENT 355

Brigand lace and silk
shade black inclinations,
opportune whispers.

FLOYD

Whole world of white fear.
What was Atlas kneeling on?
Badged brutality.

TRADE

Italian hubcaps
drive neutrality inward,
shore to coward shore.

24-HOUR NEWS CYCLE

Sad news sours the day.
Inattention to detail
fills column inches

GET 'EM IN THE FEELS

Old revolutions
burn in bloghound ad copy,
resurface for likes.

DAYLIGHT SAVINGS

Applause for accord.
A hundred heads think as one
to dictate the sun.

CHAVEZ AND THE LITTLE BLACK BIRD

A just cause rises
to baked dust and Teamster bats,
words reserved for filth.

TED

Judgment loses weight
in the morning-after fog,
then comes back swingin'.

LONELY POLITICS

All we have to give:
bleeding hearts and chiding fear
of shiny name tags.

ARLINGTON

Tears as a soft gift.
Liberty's restful children,
Robert E. Lee's ghost.

REDDIT LEAGUE ASSEMBLE

Revolt with weak thumbs.
Attack the doomed autarky
on your new iPhone.

SHACTMAN

Max fights the good fight.
No iron-fisted tank lore.
Just good sense. Hard work.

MITT

Sharp ties fold early.
Morals can get you nowhere,
booed by your own kind.

YANG

Back to the whiteboard,
new math in empowered ink,
air-dried solutions.

DEMOCRATIZE MONEY

Utility stands
tests of decentralized time,
brave altcoin envoys.

GIDEON V. WAINWRIGHT

The land of the what?
All people merit justice,
their own day in court.

HOWE

Honor is a verb.
Sundered harbors, frail motives
stoking the barred flame.

LYING IN STATE

Death quiets nothing.
Lincoln's moldering old soul
still hollers at dusk.

On Founding Documents
& Floundering Fathers

No man who ever held the office of president would congratulate a friend on obtaining it.

-John Adams

The pay is good and I can walk to work.

-John F. Kennedy

THE PREAMBLE

We the people claim
unattainable virtue
and our best guesses.

ARTICLE I

For now, heed wisdom
and good Connecticut men,
soft compromises.

ARTICLE II

Heaven's star on Earth,
though he shall from time to time
invite God to laugh.

ARTICLE III

Law and equity,
noble claims we often yield
for beauty pageants.

ARTICLE IV

Borders, birthright lines
demand ink, equal legroom,
full faith and credit.

ARTICLE V

Sharpen erasers.
How often do we shoot wide,
fully miss the mark?

ARTICLE VI

Pulpits breed discord.
Anglicans and deists
make poor dance partners.

ARTICLE VII

An overnight hack job.
Myths of unanimity
thrive in Delaware.

GENERAL WASHINGTON

Freedom's golden babe.
Born with glittering shoulders,
yoked with precedent.

JOHN ADAMS

Astonished victor
promises civility.
Always second place.

DECLARATION

Jefferson's pen leads.
Sweeping prose rattles floorboards,
gets the world moving.

MADISON

Fatherly veto.
An era of good feelings
subject to review.

MONROE DOCTRINE

More southern fervor.
Humidity makes madmen --
madmen with rifles.

CORRUPT BARGAINER

John Quincy Adams,
son of a Federalist...
slithers like one, too.

ANDREW JACKSON

Tennessee fire,
stoked beneath pioneer hooves,
burning for revenge.

FREE SOIL

Van Buren won't stand
for stale freedom. We need change,
a gardener's touch.

TIPPECANOE

Death comes easiest,
war heroes notwithstanding,
in the simple cold.

TYLER SWEARS IN

No freedom hall here.
No famed bells, no maddened crowds.
Just a hotel room.

POLK

Tangible progress:
Andy Jackson's best designs
and a Western war.

TAYLOR'S POPULAR APPEAL

Here is solid proof
Virginians fare well out west.
Let's send ev'ry one.

FILLMORE'S NEW AGENDA

It's not what was said,
but the bastards who said it.
Blank slates bring good cheer.

FRANKLIN PIERCE

Bringin' what y'all want:
sulfur, brimstone, fresh violence.
Pulpits bleed results.

LAME DUCKS AND CERTAIN WAR

A bold prediction:
James Buchanan will wear
stolid blame forever.

THE GENTLEMAN FROM ILLINOIS

Humble showmanship.
Rehearsed honor and tall words.
Stature reigns supreme.

ANDREW JOHNSON'S NEW UNION

Sympathy fishing,
he preaches a ragged line.
Friendship of all things.

GRANT'S BROKEN PROMISES

Dreaming of calm hearts.
Tired blood, second chances,
heartbreak in the hills.

RUTHERFORD

Shadows are damning.
Scrambling for light on your way
to be forgotten.

GARFIELD

Make Ohio proud.
Let them tend their own gardens,
reap what we've all sewn.

SEABORNE

You'll find Arthur there,
plucking the spring lines in tune,
surveying his reach.

GOLD

Why bury your hands
to find Earth's least-loved daughter?
Cleveland won't settle.

BENJAMIN HARRISON

Take that! Now, bury full
your face in your failed attempts.
Blood is on my side!

THE RETURN OF GROVER CLEVELAND

Railroads are like veins.
Iron is the only thing
that keeps them pumping.

MCKINNLEY KILLED IN BUFFALO

Sometimes a mere place
adds insult to injury.
The damage is done.

THEODORE

An unlikely voice
often speaks loudest, saving
soil in huge fistfuls.

TAFT VS BRYAN

Justice has its day.
Big ambitions have no place
in small, shaven men.

WILSON'S FOURTEEN POINTS FOR COMMON PEACE

If only men could count
to the end of their fingers,
the property's edge.

THE MARION STAR

Harding hardly counts.
Hayseed turned newspaper man?
We need a leader.

CALVIN

Men who say little
wield wisdom. A new age comes
one choice at a time.

WICKERSHAM COMMISSION

Reports show violence,
broken bottles and mad men
shouting Hoover's name.

FDR

Infamy withstands
tests of time. Some names echo
rev'rently onward.

TRUMAN BRINGS PEACE

Some sins burn so hot
they can't cool in heaven, where
they still count the dead.

IKE

Seas split wide open
when Kansas boys start to dream.
Oh, how dangerous!

JFK'S LEGACY

Middling at best, yet
history honors its dead
with undue treasures.

GREAT SOCIETY

Johnson says Texas
is no home for old hatreds.
Wages war abroad.

NIXON AND MAO

Tiananmen square
erupts in statecraft ballet,
handshakes change the world.

NEXT IN LINE

Ford loves a tough act
to follow and to forgive.
Pardons can come cheap.

CARTER

Gentle hands grow tired.
Long hours and lonely nights
making peace, not friends.

RAY GUN

You can see iron walls,
even from the Sunshine state,
falling fast and loud.

SENIOR

Steady hands guide ships.
Vision is a luxury
when the shore's so close.

BILL

All I remember:
camera flashes and lies.
Naught can be undone.

W

Tragedy hits home.
We briefly walk together.
Hands break to make war.

OBAMA SAYS HOPE A LOT

Brave verbs fall fecund.
Is this what real hope looks like?
Eight years of next time.

45

America's great
at inventing history.
Say "again" again.

UNCLE JOE

Expectant breath holds
only to cough, gag, deflate.
Stark disappointment.

TO THE ELECTORATE

Familiar feels good,
but what man returns to feed
a wild, biting dog?

WHEN I'M PRESIDENT

I'll burn the house down,
turn access codes to ploughshares,
probably resign.

TERM LIMITS

Forego the defense
of experience, its smell.
It's what got us here.

Timothy Tarkelly is a teacher, debate coach, activist, and poet from Southeast Kansas. He's authored several collections of poetry including *Gently In Manner, Strongly In Deed: Poems On Eisenhower* (2019), *On Slip Rigs and Spiritual Growth* (2021), *Ordering Dumplings With Bitcoin* (2022). Most recently, he collaborated with the artist Elena Samarsky on a collaborative work entitled, *All Other Forms of Expression* from OAC Books. When he's not writing and campaigning, he's getting skunked at the lake and teaching students who are far more talented than he will ever be.

This project was made possible, in part, by generous support from the Osage Arts Community.

Osage Arts Community provides temporary time, space and support for the creation of new artistic works in a retreat format, serving creative people of all kinds — visual artists, composers, poets, fiction and nonfiction writers. Located on a 152-acre farm in an isolated rural mountainside setting in Central Missouri and bordered by ¾ of a mile of the Gasconade River, OAC provides residencies to those working alone, as well as welcoming collaborative teams, offering living space and workspace in a country environment to emerging and mid-career artists. For more information, visit us at www.osageac.org

Osage Arts Community

www.ingramcontent.com/pod-product-compliance
Lightning Source LLC
Chambersburg PA
CBHW031243120626
46545CB00007B/2624